Ten Counties Away

poems by

J. Todd Hawkins

Finishing Line Press
Georgetown, Kentucky

Ten Counties Away

For Shannon

Copyright © 2017 by J. Todd Hawkins
ISBN 978-1-63534-269-7 First Edition
All rights reserved under International and Pan-American Copyright Conventions.
No part of this book may be reproduced in any manner whatsoever without written permission from the publisher, except in the case of brief quotations embodied in critical articles and reviews.

ACKNOWLEDGMENTS

I offer heartfelt gratitude to the following publications in which some of these pieces first appeared:
American Literary Review—"Oil Field Girls"
Anthology Magazine—"West of Key West"
Antietam Review—"Running Away from Home"
Aries—"Hi Jolly" and "Blind Willie Johnson"
Borderlands: Texas Poetry Review—"Ghost Dancers"
Bearing the Mask: Southwestern Persona Poems—"Death Smells like Cinnamon," "For the Correction of History," and "Papers in a Vanishing Room"
The Distillery—"Ranch at Star Mountain"
Red River Review—"Teasers Cabaret"
Southwestern American Literature—"In a Coma, Bob Wills Dreams of His Fiddle" and "Magdalena Eulogizes Her Outlaw"
Sugared Water—"November Missing" and "On the Glories of Graffiti"
Texas Poetry Calendar—"Hill Country Hesperides" (2016), "It Don't Matter Who's in Austin" (2014), "Osage Friendship Blanket, Late Nineteenth Century" (2015), "Pecos Bill, Aiming" (2013), "Prayer for a Calf" (2012), and "Waiting Inland for the Hurricane" (2011)

Thanks, too, to the editors of the Dallas Poet's Community anthology *Cattlemen and Cadillacs*, the Austin Poetry Society's *Best Austin Poetry 2010-2011*, *The Copperfield Review*, *Texas Poetry Calendar* (2018) and Lamar University Press's *Texas Weather Anthology* in which some of these pieces were republished.

"Papers in a Vanishing Room" contains found elements; the italicized and indented stanzas consist of text from the January 4, 1905, issue of the *Tishomingo News* (Oklahoma).

Publisher: Leah Maines
Editor: Christen Kincaid
Cover Art: Gable White
Author Photo: J. Todd Hawkins
Cover Design: Elizabeth Maines

Printed in the USA on acid-free paper.
Order online: www.finishinglinepress.com
        also available on amazon.com

Author inquiries and mail orders:
Finishing Line Press
P. O. Box 1626
Georgetown, Kentucky 40324
U. S. A.

Table of Contents

Pecos Bill, Aiming 1
In a Coma, Bob Wills Dreams of His Fiddle 2
Prayer for a Calf 3
November Missing 4
Osage Friendship Blanket, Late Nineteenth Century 5
Running Away from Home 6
Oil Field Girls 7
Teasers Cabaret 8
On the Glories of Graffiti 9
It Don't Matter Who's in Austin 10
Hill Country Hesperides 11
Waiting Inland for the Hurricane 12
West of Key West 13
Time among the Mustangs 14
Ghost Dancers 15
Papers in a Vanishing Room 16
Hi Jolly 18
Blind Willie Johnson 19
Rope Walker 20
Death Smells like Cinnamon 21
For the Correction of History 23
The Hymn of the Blameless Life 25
One in the Hand, or So What If Your Goose Lays
 Golden Eggs 27
Ranch at Star Mountain 29
Magdalena Eulogizes Her Outlaw 30

PECOS BILL, AIMING

I decided that night to love you,
there in the company cantina,
your calico dress still damp
from riding that catfish up the Rio.
You blushed through the barroom dust,
and all night we danced
without moving.
Perhaps it was the quicksilver
seeping from the cinnabar,
but that night I let you tame me.

Oh, how we would lie awake
under miles of our days—
wrapped in our days like blankets,
warmed by their softness—
buried in our days, unable to sense
the sun above.

I showed you how to saddle a twister
turn rattler to lariat, panther to steed.
You taught me to sweeten my breath
with wildflower honey,
your eyes glowing like phlox on fire.

They laughed when Widow-Maker threw you,
the iron hoops under your wedding gown
sending you bounding higher and higher—
so I shot the dirty cusses down.
Still, for three days, four nights,
I tried to catch you.
Only I knew you had begun your slow starving.
Only I knew you were trying to pluck the stars,
the ones you had promised me.

IN A COMA, BOB WILLS DREAMS OF HIS FIDDLE
Fort Worth, 1975

I am the oak. And you: the through-running wind.
And together we are music, my green ceaseless limbs,
your chiming invisible lapping.
I am the lighthouse keeper and you are the coast.
I am the mouth across your scar, long and hungry.

And when this song-road ends,
you will be the horse of my ghost
as we listen to the wounds of night,
to the sprawling farmlands smoking
and plows resting broken along the way.

So long past alone, we will ride.
We will ride beyond home, back to our folks' remains
back to towns ruined by the reach of our tongues
back until all differences disappear:
a boy and a man, a violin and a big Appaloosa.

And all the music salvaged, survived
will ride too, as ash through stomping hooves
as the jangle of reins and bridle
and as the quiet breath of man and horse
with their backs against sleep.

PRAYER FOR A CALF

The summer bubbled fire ants and burdock thorns
and glistened in waves dappled
by the shadows of buzzards.
We watched the stock tank inch down
and preferred to talk about box scores and neighbors' daughters
over the rainless sermons of weathermen.
We drove ten counties north for good hay,
something free of local briars and shreds of baling wire,
our old pickup hemorrhaging gasoline with every mile of road.

When the calf was born,
we managed to muster a feint of optimism,
at least in the comparative cool of morning
over bacon and good thick coffee.
But the mother we knew was over-equipped:
her teats swelled to the size of beer cans,
and the calf could find no way to nurse.

We had seen this with her before:
this cruel genetic curse.
She was a good cow,
but was poorly suited for motherhood.
So as the days got on,
we closed our windows at night,
choosing silence over coolness.

Soon, we'd drive the fences
and find the thirsty leather remains
and all our eyes would become stone,
as the pasture became caliche.
But for days, we offered silent prayers
for a calf to turn snake, unhinge its gentle jaws,
and take in the warm, wet sustenance
we hoped our world could offer.

NOVEMBER MISSING

Early that morning I went out with the misted shotgun
into the tall alleys of Granddaddy's sorghum,
stamping flat the scabbard yuccas
to which the frost stuck like stars
fallen from the leonids.

The dove flushed from the mesquite in a delicate frenzy
of panicked twigs, thorns, like a gray torch.
I shouldered the gun, fired,
and missed
mostly.

Beating the scrub, I looked for the wounded bird,
cutting and digging and ripping hands raw,
hoping to reach it before the fire ants did.

While deep inside the clutching thicket,
its death danced on papery wings,
and its hairlike bloodstrings

streaked bright the pale oak leaves
even in the beginning of rain.

OSAGE FRIENDSHIP BLANKET, LATE NINETEENTH CENTURY
Houston Museum of Natural History

The flood left them nothing, save one blanket, which they found deep in the bottoms and pulled from rot-wood and corneas of bottle ends, worming in the wet red earth. At that, not even a useful blanket. A wearing blanket, it was called, the kind an Osage girl would drape over her shoulders just so, such that each colorful silk ribbon would flow down her forearms.

> in the fresh cut bank
> the river has opened
> rain lilies, old graves

They washed it till its yellows glowed like Easter, till its blues shone brighter than the kerosene lamps above the river. When the cold came, Grandfather sold the blanket to the museum man, and they lived off that for a while.

That winter was warmed only by fever. They were quarantined, and Grandfather chopped the broomstick into checkers, built a gun from a drainpipe and a nail to keep from going mad. At least that's what I was told.

> gray morning
> possession vine choking
> the rusted harrow

I was merely ten when we drove to Houston to see it. I just remember scrawling furiously on the back of the Waffle House menu, taking back our blanket with spears of cornflower, dandelion, raw umber, and Indian red lying about me in mounds of broken wax.

> primrose unfolds
> the moth stops to drink
> its yellow dust

RUNNING AWAY FROM HOME

Inside the rest stop, Sis spent the change on Cheetos,
a lottery ticket, and a map of a place where we were not going.

Wasting for want of a seventy-song jukebox,
she had arranged our departure consulting only clouds
seen with the silos and feedlots
from atop our still pumpjack,
the one she had insisted we paint bright green,
so to seem like a giant sleeping grasshopper.

She then stole the keys to the '82 Fairmont
and we were gone.

I boot-heeled the toilet's flush plunger,
checked myself in the mirror by the condom dispenser,
and remembered what Jose Longoria told me when we were five:
the lies about Spanish cuss words and women's body parts
and how stars were so big that just one could cover
the whole back pasture.

Outside again, Sis and I searched for the highway, and night fell
with the sound of jays screaming as raccoons ate their eggs.

How we laughed nervously under sugary stars
when, as we burned the onramp in fumes of smoke and creosote,
I said this night was so much like the one
when Dad caught that cottonmouth in the backyard,
and we didn't sleep good for weeks,
squeezed tight in dream coils of snake vengeance.

OIL FIELD GIRLS
after Oil Field Girls *by Jerry Bywaters, 1940*

They walked to the road,
and the morning light fell around them,
as if the air holding it
were gift paper peeled slowly back.

The road seemed wide and steady there
but, further down the draw,
it squirmed and shook
in lazy waves of heat.

They stopped on the shoulder,
watched the dust settle
back into its place
inside their footprints.

They may have envied it, the dust,
its having a place
while they drifted
along the road

and every road
like the long-forgotten sound of water:
ghosts of something that never lived:
ghosts of ghosts.

Yet, they knew the dust, too, drifted.
They knew it sometimes rose
high in painful, cutting gusts
in clouds mighty enough to blacken day.

TEASERS CABARET

the dawn, pill-bottle orange,
falls on the highway

its light lands on lost
glass and johnson grass

crumbling together
into blacktop parking lot

grasshoppers rattle chitinous wings,
skeleton castanets

heard just by the sheetmetal mudflap girl
in silhouette above the red door

inside, at a three-legged table
hunger wrestles off

its leather straps
it convulses in gagging witchtrial fashion

upon the floor, stage, the mirrored ceiling,
and about the pole—

from beneath the day's first drink—
from behind the cracks in her eyes,

the last dancer
writes her hope in beer sweat

and then looks up
into neon and ashtray morning,

looks up crazy-eyed
as if she has done something unforgivable

ON THE GLORIES OF GRAFFITI

On the long weathered fence near the work-route stoplight above a circumscribed, inverted, five-pointed star, thick black paint with pitchforking drips reads SATIN RULES. Perhaps the Devil is not picky about disciples' spelling, but I like to picture some child, having crept from bedroom window, hunkered near a buttress of newly dead leaves laughing crazy-eyed while ducking headlights, risking grounding and years of impossible curfews to bring smirks to bleary-eyed commuters and extol the virtues of soft bedsheets: some imp conscripted in the service of angels sacrificing the plain wooden regularity to fashion a billboard that makes men clutching crumpled pinkslips feel smarter than someone. Bless the clever scribe who risked so much to make this dawn's coffee less bitter. Were that everyone set out at night armed with rattling cans pilfered from neighbors' garages to scrawl bad puns on the fences of this town—imagine the private pleasures we all would chew before the daily heaviness begins. Here's to canonization for the Dark Lord's semiliterate servants! Ah, that they may inherit the Earth.

IT DON'T MATTER WHO'S IN AUSTIN

Up from the slouching clapboard walls,
we rise, kicking tin ceiling tiles, glass.
Who would shoot at such a place?
she asks, plugging holes with her artist's fingers.
I do not answer her, turning over a church-keyed can
its red rust sticking to my fingers like sugar.
Over there must have been the stage
and that must be where they danced.

My grandfather said he once hopped a train
from Henryetta to Sherman to see the Texas Playboys.
The oilfields and cedar brakes streamed by
the slats in the boxcar,
the smell of sweat and pomade in his nose,
and a week's pay rolled tight
in the breast pocket of his town shirt.

The wind shifts, slapping thistles
against the walls of wormholed pine.
It whistles like a high lonesome bow dragging
across catgut strings. It sings
a dreamy-eyed waltz.
Step back here, through the weeds.
Take one last look.

Back in the car, we talked
about where we'd like to be buried
while the waves of yellow hawkweed rolled.

HILL COUNTRY HESPERIDES

That summer when for weeks it rained,
and the snakes streamed flooded, warm, brazen,
we fancied ourselves a sort of gang
and lived off Big Red and watermelon.
One night, we stole out from our beds
to Jackson's lot on the Santa Fe tracks.
We wrote a note and placed it there. It read,
"One melon in your patch now contains Ex-Lax."
We stole three melons, their pale green rinds glistening,
and thought our prank the best in Bell County.
We looked forward to future fruit poachings
now that Jackson's lot was our private pantry.
Next night, we found a new note in the dew.
It read, "Let's call it even. Now there're two."

WAITING INLAND FOR THE HURRICANE

In the morning, gray and distant,
there will be coffee and the waves
of a child's laughter when the images
of inundation give way
to Saturday morning cartoons.
Then, they say, will come the wind, rain.

We will meddle nervously, bearing
the uneasy silence of pretended calm
as we hang old sepia family pictures
in the stairway.

Those grim faces from behind decades
of storms and loss will stare
and judge their progenies' faith.

We will know the places they show
on the news. We will have strolled
their sunny seawalls and tasted their ice creams,
soft like rainbows must be.

We will know it is futile to tie this world together
with chain link fences and swing sets.

Perhaps we will lose the young oak
we struggled all summer to free of fungus.
Perhaps we will lose more.

But now, the house only sleeps
and the wind chime
only whispers the delicate peals
of painful anticipation.

WEST OF KEY WEST

the lanterns along the pier were impatient by twilight
glinting off lacquered swells, gem-red, gem-green

while she stared to the gulf
past the silken blue seam
of unbroken horizons
and walked out slowly
until the sea
took her legs,
her oiled shoulders,
safely, the way screen doors in summer
permit only a perfect breeze

she was alone in the ocean
searching out the moon:

even when we were naked,
she still wanted to be skinless

moonsick ghostcrabs
bled through seafoam
onto sugary beaches a second before
being dragged back to the breast of earth

we are precious   *now*, I tried to explain

yet even awash in ocean tide
sand somehow finds a way inside

TIME AMONG THE MUSTANGS

We are shaken by each wave. Far off, jetties crawl with whitecaps. Shards of sand fly, tormenting even shelled things and diamondbacks with hooded eyes. We have just the fragile grasses to anchor us together. Still, they say the island moves inches more every year as sand from one end is taken away, added to other places.

> laguna madre—
> ghost crabs in tide pools
> watch waves rise

When the Spanish were shipwrecked here, their frightened horses ran wild upon the beach, scavenged the dunes. For generations, their descendants roamed these shores, untamed as the wind that bore their fathers.

> shell midden
> unearthed by the storm
> glows white as the moon

But even they are gone now, mere shadows of manes, bones stroked white by salt. Even they are gone now, leaving only us and squadrons of birds whose names I'll never learn.

> driftwood-lined trail
> leading inland through dunes
> from lead-colored shore

GHOST DANCERS
after Breaking Camp *by Henry F. Farny, 1891*

"Up to and including 1880 the country had a frontier of settlement, but at present the unsettled area has been so broken into by isolated bodies of settlement that there can hardly be said to be a frontier line."
—Bulletin of the Superintendent of the Census for 1890

They leave in the mystery
of the yellow dawn.
Their spiry tents
have fallen,
Their fires,
gone.

The prairie softly
fades in snow
lost in whiteness—
the bison also
lost, skulls clipped
clean by crows.

A country no longer here,
this is only paint. It is dust,
this fictional frontier. And still
they drag travois in whiteness
nowhere: peaceably if they will—
forcefully if they must.

PAPERS IN A VANISHING ROOM

In January 1905, Sylvia Ridley, a Choctaw woman, was sent from Oklahoma to the Hiawatha Asylum for Insane Indians in South Dakota. Confinement at the asylum was often used as retribution against mentally healthy Native Americans who had irritated Indian agents or local politicians. Even for the standards at the time, conditions were deplorable at the institution, where inmates were restrained for extended periods, forced to live in filth, and denied basic needs. In June, Ridley died. She is buried in the old asylum cemetery, which is today located between the fourth and fifth fairways of the Hiawatha Golf Club.

1905. Durant, Choctaw Nation, Ind. Terr.
Dearest K—

You'll remember, I used to draw butterflies
where I wanted to cut. Not anymore.
Maybe you have heard

> The Sulphur Post *Says SYLVIA RIDLEY INSANE*
> *Sylvia Ridley, an Indian woman of 35 years of age,*
> *became violently insane Tuesday. She was taken*
> *to Ardmore under arrest. She was tried Monday,*
> *January 2, at Marietta, and sent to the asylum.*

I am getting well. Just this morning, I woke
and for a moment thought I was home (but then
all in a panic because I could not find the children).
At night: I imagine the smell of our squash blossoms filling my
    room.
Then, my hands and my mouth and my throat and my wrists
peel open, unwhorl like squash blossoms—
my ears go off, my eyes, my fingers float away.
From the holes flow the moons you taught me to name,
moons sifting across the white floors
shadow patterns, as precise as spiders':
the green corn moon, the worm moon,
the beautiful long nights moon.

> *The woman had been married three times; her first two husbands, Indians, died, and Ridley, a white man, left her, got a divorce, and married again. It is supposed that worry over these facts led to her dementia.*

For years, our people wandered carrying the bones of their dead
until they found a place to lay them.
Even today, we are returned home,
placed upon a litter, covered in skins and bark,
provisioned with food and drink, a killed dog
for companionship. And after some weeks,
the bone-picker comes and scrapes the flesh away
with his long fingernails. So we can always know this.

> *She had been about Sulphur for the last four or five months, working at one place and another, but never staying long.*

All I said was that I know there is God, but
I also think to grandmother's stories of Nalusa chito,
the Great Black Thing, how if I gave into the sadness,
Nalusa chito would crawl through my skin and eat my soul.
Do you remember when you would laugh at me for crying?
I forgive you for that now.
There is a woman here who frightens me.
Her name is Yells-at-Night.
I believe I will see you soon.

Love, S.R.

HI JOLLY

Syrian Hadji Ali arrived at Indianola, Texas, in 1856 with thirty-three camels, purchased for the Army's new U.S. Camel Corps. The camels were brought to support supply routes in the Southwest, and Ali, whose name was soon anglicized to "Hi Jolly," had been hired to teach soldiers how to use them. Despite the camels' demonstrated usefulness, the soldiers hated them, and by the eve of the Civil War, they had all been sold or released. Years later, in 1903, a 75-year-old Ali sat in a saloon in Quartzite, Arizona, when a prospector rushed in, talking of an enormous camel just outside town. Ali stood and left. Several weeks afterward, his body was found in the desert, his arms wrapped around the neck of what may have been the last camel in the Southwest.

Were not my throat a knotted cord of drizzled glass
or my legs twigs of ant-gnawed wood, waiting to betray!
Ah, then I might gain that distant, doomful bray
and pray with another sad brute that quickly life may pass
into human leather spanning Shinbone Crevasse.
But the prints upon which jagged buzzard-shadows play
fade in this light, and toothy mouths seek untroublesome prey
as sand-scarred and thorny things punish my bold trespass.
Only just over that peak—though my feet split like burst
    wineskins—
must lie my serai among date palms and emerald oases.
Before full dark, I'll have slipped there like a sparrow past trammels
to hold opulent feasts with fellow caliphs and sultans.
There I'll eat roasted lamb and lick honey from backs of bees.
I'll rest in the arms of Allah, then ride to heaven, carried by camels.

BLIND WILLIE JOHNSON

Around 1905, seven-year-old Willie Johnson was permanently blinded when his step-mother, angered at his father's infidelity, threw lye in the boy's face. As an adult, he embarked on a career in music, spent on the street corners and in the Baptist churches of Beaumont, Texas. A recording session in Dallas produced some of the most popular religious music of the era due to the appeal of Johnson's vigorous pocketknife slide guitar style, his gravelly false bass, and a penchant for making the holy sound secular, for using the blues idiom to convey the Word. Around 1945, Johnson survived his house's catching fire, yet he slept on wet bedding and contracted pneumonia. As his illness progressed, he sought treatment at the hospital in Beaumont, but was denied admission. He died shortly afterwards.

Sheep, sheep, can you find your way home, through briar-
gored fields, searching blind with no eyes to see hell,
with no breath to speak God, where men belch sin-fire
to whiskey-minded women? Didn't I lead you well?

Outside Saint James Infirmary with night's clientele—
whoresmen and hustlers who've sinned and defiled,
done wrong all their lives—I sang as the Jezebel,
the Cain, the Judas rebuked Jesus' mercy mild.

Though I know: Sunday's wind pricks like a fretting hand
while the dark strums him raw, even for one who's reviled
Saturday's gin every day he's breathed. And farmland
loved and nurtured like the Lord's own Child,

can bring forth rock for a lifetime haul.
How the Lord sometimes makes a Job of us all!

ROPE WALKER

On July 28, 1898, in Corsicana, Texas, a group of merchants sponsored a publicity stunt to attract local farmers to town. They hired a one-legged transient tight-wire walker to walk a rope stretched over Beaton Street from the tops of two downtown buildings. The sixty-nine-year-old man had a peg leg with a groove notched in it to accommodate the wire, and to add to the spectacle, he was to carry a cast-iron stove on his back. When he was halfway across the street, the rope sagged too much, and he fell. Dying, he told those attending to him his place and date of birth, but if he gave his name, no one remembered it. He was buried in the Corsicana cemetery under a marker engraved simply, "Rope Walker."

I have a scar from some spill from when I was young,
too young to even remember. But I've spent hot days mulling over
how raw underskin must've glowed, how blood-seeds must've
    clung
to the sparkling shards of some bud vase, and how it must've made
    me braver.

Till I was old enough to know better, I imagined invisible
    shoemakers
pushing through elves to sew my screaming shut with shoestring,
perhaps a poultice of rotted swamp moss, and a handful of
    jawbreakers.
Then the Fire of '55 took my wife, my leg, and I met real suffering.

So I spent forty years walking rope from one jerkwater town
to the next, sometimes skating like Christ on the Lake of
    Gennesaret,
thinking if I ever stumbled, I'd sink as slowly as thistledown,
because I was bound to have had all the hurt that I was ever gonna
    get.

You just need to know I was born in '29 in Princeton, New Jersey,
and that life permits a few small slips, but it's damn hard on the
    clumsy.

DEATH SMELLS LIKE CINNAMON

In November 1882 in Total Wreck, Arizona, a disagreement broke out between businessman E.B. Salsig and John Drummond over the sale of a mine. Drummond called Salsig into the street to resolve the quarrel. Once outside, Salsig punched Drummond, who then drew on and shot Salsig. One bullet struck him in the chest, but was stopped by a wallet filled with a thick bundle of love letters that Salsig was carrying, saving his life.

In the carnival tintype you looked like a promise.
The painted background . . . I memorized the lines,
each like a twilight desert path to water.

I told you I would keep it forever. I even thought
I might. But that afternoon . . . imagine! . . .
there was the crack

(small, really) and then the sun became a candle
slim, wavering, and its center:
the bright fiery kiss of a cigar tip to skin.

I believe I lay there a long time.
I imagined the scent of death: hot, sweet, woody—
like cinnamon. You must think I am mad:

Everywhere here are men buried inside rocks
and in the spaces between the grains of sand:
the Mexican woodcutters shot last week by Geronimo's men

and the horse thieves we hung and hung and hung again
from the windmill derrick until
the water went foul. We mine ore

from their bones every day. And I know
one day my name will be lost among theirs.
Yet, at that moment, all I could picture

were the words that were gone, your words lost behind
that hole, vanished forever in a great silent ellipsis.
Only then did I really want to kill him, to dash him wetly on stones.

In the shadow and dirt, as the men gathered round,
wheezing dust and blood, I reached up,
touched the bullet in my breast

pocket. And it came to me: perhaps they were not really lost—
maybe they were forced clean through,
your script now written in me.

Perhaps the letters now swirled within:
the flourished E's inside my lungs,
stray legs of perfumed R's rising in my blood.

Women gasped when I took the parcel from my pocket,
blood soaked like a holy thing. And from the road I rose,
smiled, looked about for a fast horse.

FOR THE CORRECTION OF HISTORY

In 1903, a Shakespeare-quoting drifter named David George committed suicide in Enid, Oklahoma, but not before confessing to being Abraham Lincoln's assassin, John Wilkes Booth. George's body was embalmed and placed on display at the Enid funeral parlor until it could be claimed by the government or his nearest kin. The mummy became an Enid tourist attraction and eventually fell into the hands of William Evans, "Carnival King of the Southwest," who exhibited the Booth mummy throughout the West for many years as a carnival attraction.

Yes, the six-legged sheep and the dog-faced calf
are lovely in their way. But for you, something . . . different.
Let me tell you this: I have a mummy.
Come closer, yes, closer. . . .
He is real, and you may see him for yourself
for just two bits. Look:

the brow scar, a misplaced sword blow from *Richard III*;
the crooked thumb, crushed in a curtain windlass long ago;
and of course the twisted leg, so crudely set by Dr. Mudd.
I know each crease. I comb his moustache, polish his marble eyes.
And at night, I slick his leather limbs with Vaseline
till he glistens like scarab wings in a black desert.

I sleep next to him in the panel truck,
we two showmen, we two curators of dead legends.
These days, I never leave his side.
For once in San Diego, he was kidnapped, ransomed,
and in Salt Lake City, I fled in the dark—
the sheriff after me for teaching a false history.

In Big Spring, they fined me for harboring a corpse.
They tried to bury my Johnny. As if their own lives
were so genuine; their own stupid stories, veritable.
It is enough to make me want to stay out here forever, to show
my relics before the cactus cloaked in powdered stone,
the buzzards minding their private bones.

Yes, even the damn buzzards would be better audience—
I hit one on the way here as it gorged on day-dead rabbit,
swollen with heat, and it splashed into unwashable crevices of the
    Ford.
I cursed and laughed for miles. But the final laugh is theirs,
for any way out of here or into here feels forever gone now,
and the buzzards, from the ground, are sublime and holy.

Or perhaps I will learn to float with them
through yellow rivers of dust in sun,
dancing with the cottonwood plumes,
and leave my two-faced kitten—precious Janus!—
my pickled punks and feegee mermaid,
and, yes, even my Booth—

Leave him there, on the roadside, the withered pharaoh,
Leave him, clothed in corroborations, dressed in affidavits,
propped on plywood
for the correction of history.
Leave him here, disentranced
with his own pretended permanence.

THE HYMN OF THE BLAMELESS LIFE

We dug with our hands, my brother and I. To loose the dun dirt among the stone. Almost secretly we nested seeds, two here, three there. Each pit a tender cup. We buried our father in every one.

The delicate flute song, the thin peals of el pitero, they came to us. They squirmed in crags of cliffs. Beyond, they flowered over hills, lilting, blooming. They sounded like a small death passing through reeds. Like a whisper hating its own breath. Like a scream under a trusted palm.

The Hermanos de Luz. The Bothers of Light. The Penitentes. A secretive sect in these parts. Known for self-flagellation. Once we plucked the amole weed and yucca strands from which they fashioned their short whips. Our father would take them and return home from the morada stiff and sore.

Lots were drawn on Ash Wednesday. And on Good Friday, they tied one brother to the largest cross and hoisted him up. The pito sounding the same tone a thousand ways. We had heard the stories, how those who died on the cross were buried in secret. La encomendación del alma chanted over his gray remains, stiffening in the bright heat. How only his boots would be left outside his family's home.

High and light, the flute stabbed the sunlit pillars of dust. We dug deeper and deeper and deeper until our fingers split whole. When the priests left, it fell to the brothers to bring the faith. In the absence of sacraments, a crucifixion will do—a crucifixion and a song.

In the dark, we walked home from the fields, raw from sun, my brother and I. We walked through the cactus, spines sticking our legs and feet. At home, in the cool adobe shadows, we left our shoes by the door. In our mouths, there was the wet-dust taste of rain that would never arrive. We chewed it slowly watching the light leave the sky. Greasewood always lies of rain. We had grown so tired of hearing it speak.

>   in the churchyard
>   where we searched for you:
>   the pito's song

>   dreams of lightning
>   then remembering nothing
>   but waking up

>   the dimming stars
>   wingtips graze leaves
>   even the owl is lost

ONE IN THE HAND,
OR SO WHAT IF YOUR GOOSE LAYS GOLDEN EGGS

There was first the pinch,
Brief, yes, but it hurt like hell.
I reached up and felt the warm blood,
oily between my fingertips.
Then I made the frantic call
to the veterinarian.
The prognosis was not good.
Apparently,
when one's pet chicken
plucks one's diamond earring
from one's ear—and swallows it—
difficult decisions must be made.
I stared in Henrietta's vacant eyes
holding her feathered head gently
in my hands like Yorick's skull.
To fricassee—
or not to fricassee?
That is the question.
For days I did what I could:
purgatives, diarrhetics . . .
I pored over newspapers
looking for iridescence
in old car ads and op-eds
like a miner panning for gold.
Nothing worked.
I wondered what life I could give her,
fretting both foxes and jewel thieves.
But as I brooded over it,
I came to love her more—
knowing the setting would dissolve
over time, the platinum leaching
into her bones—
knowing the diamond would stay part of her,

glowing darkly in her gizzard
with the pea gravel from my driveway.
I resolved that the sky would not fall.
She would live out her days
the most valuable chicken in the county,
the Lamborghini of poultry,
sacred, and scarce like hen's teeth.

RANCH AT STAR MOUNTAIN

The gray air, anointed
with the mist of phlox,
broomweed, juniper

is still, locked in windmill rust,
and the fragments of this land
seep up from shadowed stones

Silence kept in barbed wire fence—
though decades unmended,
still the thorns: a perfect bind

Soundless even are scatterings of quail,
alarmed, perhaps
by the dry corn's shriveled sigh

So we must read the mysteries here
written upon the brittle soil
and make the past ourselves—
for the stray stone wall
strewn by the drywell,
for the puddle of iron nails
guarding emerald nettles,
for the phantom phone pole
dressed in garlands of copper wire . . .

We must insert some ghost here
hauling rock, clearing tree
and make it smile and suffer—

Or else gods and fiends
cast these relics
like nets to sea
to grab sad minds
wanting history!

MAGDALENA EULOGIZES HER OUTLAW
after "Romance in Durango" by Bob Dylan, 1976

night, the thoughts it makes,
not what may but what will be
one little well-aimed light
the flash, the hills, the look
your gun, and you, here quick, here slain

words say "don't: leave: me" but
mean only "come: closer: pain."
sharp, a feel they are vibrating,
the things I hear in my head
the thunder that wasn't after all

the dancing will be gone
and instead the desert will be my life
hold me, Durango, hold us
take the goddamn horse, the whole protection of god
take them, mi querida, with you

diamonds shine behind eyes
your gold earring, I saw to that, new boots—
I left the blood unwashed, for the town
and church have little in prayers for you—
the padre says nothing of our child

the coolness of night
you dreamed of
is inside bells now
and the baker's son
plays your guitar

you were right
about what's done is done,
but also wrong: living happy among ruins
and the peopling of our ghosts
with music and lovers' heat

J. Todd Hawkins was born and bred in Fort Worth, Texas. And, when it comes down to it, that has a lot to do with a lot of his writing. Billed as "Where the West Begins," Fort Worth rests on a borderland, a cultural crossroads, a liminal place where different narratives interweave. As with most places, some of these narratives were more prominent than others. There was the public image put out by civic boosters—cowboys, oil, high culture—but there was also a subversive, underground scene just as important to the functioning of the city. So Hawkins learned to listen for the quiet voices. And he grew up exploring the Fort's honky tonks as well as its punk rock clubs, its world-class art museums and its abandoned graffiti-splattered meat-packing plants. In school, he learned about its heralded native sons, while in friends' backyards, he learned about the gangsters who once prowled Jacksboro Highway. This collection reflects those dichotomies, revealing the softness of a hard people, the beauty in an arid land, the humor in tragedy, and the vitality of stories nearly forgotten.

In the early 1990s, Hawkins left Fort Worth for Austin to attend the University of Texas. At UT, he was elected to Phi Beta Kappa and graduated with a B.A. in English and psychology, after some time spent studying abroad at Oxford University. He taught special needs elementary students in a Title I East Austin school, experience which led to his current job as editor, writer, and language specialist for an educational publishing company. Later, he attended Texas Tech University, where he earned an M.A. in technical communication.

Hawkins's poetry has appeared in *AGNI, The Bitter Oleander, Modern Haiku, The Louisville Review, Bayou Magazine, Parcel, The American Literary Review, Southwestern American Literature,* and dozens of other journals. His poems are found in anthologies such as *Lifting the Sky: Southwestern Haiku and Haiga* (Dos Gatos Press, 2013), *Bearing the Mask: Southwestern Persona Poems* (Dos Gatos Press, 2016), and *Texas Weather* (Lamar University Press, 2016). He has presented and discussed poetry on panels at the University of Mississippi's Southern Writers/Southern Writing Conference, Tarleton State University's Langdon Review Arts Festival, and Oklahoma State University's Graduate Humanities Conference.

He still lives in Texas with his beloved wife Shannon—whom he has known since he was four—and his three children. When they can, they travel to lost and forgotten places, poking around abandoned buildings and cemeteries in the middle of nowhere, inventing stories. Other times, they're perfectly happy escaping to the family ranch in the valley of Star Mountain on the northern edge of the Texas Hill Country.

www.ingramcontent.com/pod-product-compliance
Lightning Source LLC
LaVergne TN
LVHW041509070426
835507LV00012B/1429